NIGHT
CREATURES

NIGHT
CREATURES

Wade Cooper

make
believe
ideas

We are the creatures of the night.
Can you see us? Take a peep.
By day you will not find us.
We are awake when you are asleep.

Can you hear us?
We are near.
We are hiding,
but we are here.

Reading together

This book is an ideal early reader for your child, combining simple words and sentences with stunning colour photography of real-life animals. Here are some of the many ways you can help your child gain confidence in reading. Encourage your child to:

- Look at and explore the detail in the pictures.
- Read each word slowly.
- Sound out unfamiliar words.
- Read and repeat each short sentence.

Look at the pictures

Make the most of each page by talking about the pictures and spotting key words. Here are some questions you can use to discuss each page as you go along:

- Why do you like this animal?
- What would it feel like to touch?
- Where does it live?
- What noise does it make?

Look at rhymes

Some of the sentences in this book are simple rhymes. Encourage your child to recognise rhyming words. Try asking the following questions:

- What does this word say?
- Can you find a word that rhymes with it?

- Look at the ending of two words that rhyme. Are they spelled the same? For example, "bright" and "tight", and "tight" and "white".

Test understanding

It is one thing to understand the meaning of individual words, but you need to check that your child understands the facts in the text.

- Play "spot the obvious mistake". Read the text as your child looks at the words with you, but make an obvious mistake to see if he or she has understood. Ask your child to correct you and provide the right word.
- After reading the facts, shut the book and make up questions to ask your child.
- Ask your child whether a fact is true or false.
- Present your child with three answers to a question and ask him or her to pick the correct one.

Quiz pages

At the end of the book there is a simple quiz. Ask the questions and see if your child can remember the right answers from the text. If not, encourage him or her to look up the answers.

Night creatures

Some animals are awake at night, and they sleep during the day. Owls and bats are awake at night. Crocodiles, foxes and jaguars are awake at night, too!

hoohooo

I have eyes
like the moon.
They sparkle at night.
I see my prey
in black and white.
I turn my head
from left to right.

Did you know?

Owls eat mice. They swallow
a mouse whole. Then they
cough up the bones and fur.

All is calm.
All is bright.
I catch my prey.
I hold on tight.
I use my beak
to crunch and bite!

Swoop

Did you know?

Owls have sharp claws to catch and hold prey.

By day I look like
moss or bark.
I open my wings
when it gets dark.

F l u t t e r

Flutter

Did you know?

Moths taste and smell
with their antennae.

I hang out in
a cave or tree.
My eyes can see,
but in the dark,
I get around
by using sound.

echo
echo
echo
echo

Did you know?

A bat's wing is like a hand with long
fingers that are covered with skin.

Munch

Did you know?

Foxes hide in dens
under the ground.

I eat chickens.

I eat eggs.

I eat anything
with legs.

I eat rabbits.

I eat mice.

I eat roots.

I eat rice.

I eat squirrels.

I eat seeds.

I eat turtles.

I eat weeds.

I'm a cat,
but I keep cool
by swimming
in a stream or pool.
I hide my food
before I eat –
monkey, deer
or turtle meat.

Did you know?

Jaguars are good
climbers and swimmers.

My fur is long
and black and white.
I walk in gardens
late at night.
If you scare me,
I will spray
a stinky smell.
So stay away!

Pooey!

Did you know?

Skunks eat insects,
mice and rubbish!

Did you know?

Bush babies live in treetops.
They eat insects, fruit, and tree gum.

Ai! Ai!

Ai! Ai!

I leap through
treetops,
way up high.
Can you hear
my baby cry?
I'm not a baby.
I'm just shy.

Ai! Ai!

23

crush

I have grey hair,
a long snout
and strong jaws.
I have black-and-white
stripes, crushing teeth
and sharp claws.

Did you know?

Badgers have strong legs and sharp claws. They dig tunnels and dens.

box

Did you know?

A baby kangaroo is tiny.
It finishes growing in a pouch
near its mother's tummy.

I'm the hopper
that loves to box.
I'm the boxer that
hops and hops.
I eat grasses
and crops.
And I hop lots.

hop

What do you know?

1. Can owls see in colour?

2. What do owls eat?

3. Why do owls have sharp claws?

4. What do moths use their antennae for?

5. Where do bats hang out?

6. How do jaguars keep cool?

7. Where does a baby kangaroo grow?

8. How do bats get around in the dark?

9. What does a skunk do
   when it is scared?

10. Where do bush babies live?

11. What colour is a badger?

12. What do foxes do
    during the day?

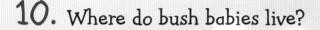

Answers

1. No. They can only see in black and white.
2. Owls eat mice. 3. Owls have sharp claws to
catch and hold prey. 4. Moths smell and taste with their antennae.
5. Bats hang out in caves and trees. 6. Jaguars swim to keep cool.
7. A baby kangaroo grows in a pouch near its mother's tummy.
8. Bats use sound to find their way in the dark. 9. When a skunk is
scared, it sprays a stinky smell. 10. Bush babies live high in the treetops.
11. A badger is grey with black-and-white stripes. 12. They hide in dens
under the ground.

Dictionary

beak
A beak is the hard part of a bird's mouth.

antennae
Lots of insects have two antennae on their head. They use them to smell and taste.

claws
Claws are the sharp nails on the feet of a bird or animal.

snout
A snout is a big animal nose. Badgers and foxes have snouts.

jaws
Jaws are at the top and bottom of the mouth. Most animals have teeth in their jaws.

Key words

Here are some key words used in context. Help your child to use other words from the border in simple sentences.

I open **my** wings.

I'm a wild **cat**.

A fox has a **big**, bushy tail.

Yes, I hop about lots.

An owl has eyes **like** the moon.